T0359474

©Jon Gamble 2019

First published in Australia in 2012 by:
Karuna Publishing
122 Church Street
Wollongong NSW 2500
Australia

All correspondence to the above address or by email to:
info@irritablebowelsyndrome.net.au

All rights reserved. No part of this book may be reproduced, stored in a retrieval system, or transmitted in any form or by any means, electronic, mechanical or otherwise, without the prior written permission of the author.

Every effort has been made to ensure that this book is free from errors or omissions. However, the author and publishers shall not accept responsibility for injury, loss or damage occasioned to any person acting or refraining from action as a result of material in this book, whether or not such injury, loss or damage is in any way due to any negligent act or omission, breach of duty or default on the part of the author or publishers.

This book is not intended to replace competent medical advice, nor is self-diagnosis recommended in the absence of adequate evaluation by a health professional. In all cases, please seek the advice of a health professional, and advise him or her of any treatment you are undergoing. The author is a health professional in private practice. The therapeutic recommendations in this book are provided only as examples of successful treatments that have been used with patients. The suggestions in this book are not suitable for patients with severe allergies that cause anaphylactic reactions.

ISBN 978-0-6484144-0-7

Treat Yourself Series

2nd Edition

Treat Your IBS Yourself
Your IBS Toolkit

Jon Gamble
BA ND Adv Dip Hom

Series Editor: Nyema Hermiston

Karuna Publishing

Contents

PART ONE
IBS Overview

PART TWO
Discover the Reason for Your IBS and How to Treat it

Appendices

Selected Bibliography

PART ONE
IBS Overview

....

I
So you have been diagnosed with Irritable Bowel Syndrome ...

....

... and you are looking for a solution for yourself, or someone close to you. All the procedures and tests have been done, your colonoscopy is normal, yet you are still searching for an answer - and some relief. Your doctor has told you that you must have Irritable Bowel Syndrome, and you must reduce your stress levels and learn to live with it.

So despite your own and your doctor's best efforts, you are left with ongoing gut pain and discomfort. You are not alone. More and more people are being diagnosed with IBS than a few decades ago, when it was scarcely known.

Having treated gut problems for 30 years now, I have learned that there are not one, but many reasons why people have IBS, meaning that there is no single solution out there going to be found.

So if the specific cause of your IBS is not identified, it is not possible for you to receive the treatment you need for your particular type of IBS. To complicate the situation, often one person has several causes of their IBS, which is why you may have had various treatments with no lasting effect over many years.

When the cause or causes of your IBS have been established, you can look forward to a far better outcome than being in the limbo state of 'managing your symptoms' as many practitioners suggest.

Contrary to popular opinion and experience, IBS can often be cured, once the underlying causes are recognised and treated accordingly.

NOTE:

Before reading this book, ensure that you have had a diagnosis of IBS from your doctor. Any abnormal bowel symptoms must be correctly diagnosed. If you've shown up all clear on your tests, then read on!

II
Quick IBS Checklist

According to the Rome III criteria,[1] classic Irritable Bowel Syndrome (IBS) refers to *shifting abdominal pain with alternating constipation and diarrhoea*, also described as 'irregular or disturbed bowel function'.

Recognise These?

IBS is diagnosed when there is ongoing abdominal pain plus two or more of these symptoms:

- Bloating
- Constipation alternating with diarrhoea
- Morning cluster of motions
- Never completely empty feeling after a bowel motion
- Pain is better after a bowel motion
- Your bowel motion changes when you have the pain.

---

1 *Rome III Criteria theromefoundation.org (last accessed 14th Feb 2019) The Rome criteria is a system developed to classify functional gastrointestinal disorders (FGIDs), disorders of the digestive system when symptoms cannot be explained by the structural or tissue abnormality, based on clinical symptoms. FGIDs include irritable bowel syndrome, functional dyspepsia, functional constipation, and functional heartburn.*

III
'Unexplained' IBS Symptoms
....

Even if you do not have the classic IBS symptoms, you may still have been given a diagnosis of IBS.

In short, people with varying (functional) gut symptoms tend to be placed in the same diagnostic barrel. This is because 'IBS' has become a vague, generic term for the presence of abdominal discomfort with variable bowel habits, when no other medical diagnosis can be found. A thorough analysis of the history and course of the condition has not been a feature of the diagnosis.

Symptoms indicating there is more to your IBS than meets the eye:

- Allergies
- Crawling skin
- Fatigue (Chronic Fatigue Syndrome sometimes accompanies IBS)
- Gastric reflux
- Headaches
- Nausea
- Restless leg syndrome
- Susceptibility to colds, flu, sinusitis or post-nasal drip
- Unexplained insomnia or disturbed sleep patterns.

IV
Lifestyle Factors

* Eating meals too quickly (thus swallowing air)
* Excess caffeine (coffee, Coke, guaraná)
* Inadequate sleep
* Inadequate water intake (dehydration)
* Lack of exercise
* Long working hours and delaying going to the toilet
* Poor nutrition
* Stress.

Diet

Large, infrequent meals put significant pressure on the digestive system, and are sometimes a factor in indigestion and reflux. Under-eating can also cause digestive disturbance. It is true that IBS improves by correcting the diet alone, but this is seldom the cure. Increasing dietary fibre can help IBS, but only if constipation is your main symptom.

Stress

IBS Is More Than Just Stress

You may have been told your IBS is stress-related. Because medical tests have not found any abnormalities, 'stress' is seen as the cause of IBS and patients are duly prescribed stress management techniques. Cognitive Behavioural Therapy (CBT), hypnosis, meditation, and improving lifestyle can all help symptoms, but only bring an end to the problem in a small number of cases.

Any symptoms can worsen from stress, so it makes sense that gut symptoms will improve with less stress. While most patients with IBS find that stress can be a trigger of their symptoms, **it is seldom the only cause of IBS.** IBS often has several causes, which may or may not be connected with emotional stress.

A lot of stress is involved with modern living. We could all do with at least half an hour each day to just 'be'. That could mean walking on the beach, drawing, patting the dog, doing some meditation, fishing, or any other single pointed activity that you find relaxing and enjoyable. Something that does not involve thinking; to escape for a little while from the mental noise machine in our heads, like music, Tai chi or Yoga, are great ways to reduce stress.

In the 25 years I have been treating IBS, I can think of only two patients whose IBS symptoms were entirely the result of emotional stress. Therefore, stress management may help your IBS but is unlikely to cure it.

In the vast majority of cases, stress is not the primary cause of IBS. Stress aggravates an underlying chronic state of inflammation or reactivity. Having made this

point, if you are under constant stress, it is difficult to heal a chronic disease like IBS unless your stress is being adequately managed.

While I recognise that emotional stress 'turns up the volume' on IBS, it is equally common for **IBS to turn up the volume on emotional stress**. One health professional has described IBS as 'somato-psychic' (as opposed to psycho-somatic).[2]

The interesting dynamic that I see, is that **once the underlying problem is corrected, the emotional stress gets better**.

V
Children and IBS
....

Children with IBS have the causes of IBS as adults. In fact, many of the origins of IBS can date from childhood. Therefore, the information provided in this book applies equally to children as it does to adults.

---

2 I am indebted to Dr Braham Rabinov for this distinction: www. yourgutfeelings.com.au Last accessed 14th February 2019

VI
Common IBS Treatments

● ●

- *Peppermint oil:* to relieve abdominal pain associated with flatulence (can worsen reflux symptoms)
- *Buscopan:* to relieve abdominal cramping
- Bulking agents, such as Psyllium husks, to improve bowel motility and constipation
- *Endep:* a small daily dose of this antidepressant reduces the pain signals the brain perceives from the signals sent by signals from the disturbed gut.
- Separate starch and protein diet: to reduce the load on digestion, and thus reduce the amount of flatulence
- *FODMAP:* a special diet to address IBS symptoms. See Appendix A
- *Iberogast:* a herbal blend which is showing promising symptom relief for both IBS and gastro-oesophageal reflux disease.

If you have tried some or all of these without much success, it's time to read on!

VII
What's Causing *Your* IBS?

••

Although IBS sufferers can have similar symptoms, the causes of those symptoms can differ, which explains why a single treatment for all IBS has never been found. The treatment needs to be **tailored to the causes.** Often, a detailed look at a patient's history reveals these causes. Here is a list of questions that **must be asked of every IBS sufferer:**

- When did your IBS symptoms start? How long ago exactly? How old were you? (If you have trouble remembering, try to remember a time when your digestion felt normal – during childhood? Was it at High School? Your first job? etc).

- What was happening when your symptoms began? Were you travelling?

- Were you sick and needed one or more courses of antibiotics?

- Were you taking other medications for a period of time?

- Did you have a bout of gastro-enteritis either at home or travelling overseas?

- Do you have any food sensitivities? Is there a family history of food sensitivity?

- Women: are you currently taking, or have you ever taken the oral contraceptive pill?

- Did a period of stress start your symptoms? This could be: moving house, relationship problems, a death in the family, work stress, and/or financial worries. See 'IBS is more than just stress' in Part I.

VIII
Tests

Sometimes **specialised** pathology tests are needed to properly diagnose the underlying reason(s) for your IBS. Your health professional can order these.

The most common specialised tests needed are:

- IgA Transglutaminase for Coeliac disease (Blood test)
- Complete Digestive Stool Analysis (Stool sample)
- Hair Mineral Analysis (Hair sample)
- IgG (Immunoglobulin G4) Food Sensitivity Panel (Blood test)
- Intestinal Permeability (Urine test).
- Oligoscan - spectrophotometry, a scan conducted during your consultation.

PART TWO
Discover the Reason
For Your IBS
and
How to Treat it

· ·

Chapter One
Intestinal Parasites

· ·

Gut parasites, both helminths (worms) and protozoa (eg giardia), are a very common cause of IBS in both children and adults. In fact, intestinal parasites are so common that one researcher states that "most of the world's 4 billion people are colonised by parasites".[3] Another study has found that 67 per cent of IBS patients improved after taking antibiotics to treat gut parasites.[4] Some sources suggest that parasitic infection renders the gut more sensitive due to the damage they cause in the gut wall.[5] These studies compel us to closely look at parasites as a major cause of IBS.

3 Dr L Galland, MD: mdheal.org/parasites.htm (last accessed 14th February 2019)

4 Borody, T, et al, "Eradication of Dientamoeba fragilis can resolve IBS-like symptoms", *Journal of Gastroenterology and Hepatology* (2002) 17 (supp) A103

5 Dr Terry Bolin www.gutfoundation.com.au (last accessed 14th February 2019)

How do gut parasites infect us?

Gut parasites can develop after:

Food poisoning
- A stomach bug while travelling overseas
- Gastroenteritis
- Drinking tank water. Bird droppings, which carry parasites, can easily enter tank water.
- Giardia and cryptosporidium can infiltrate municipal water supplies after prolonged rainfall.

Symptoms
- A wide range of symptoms are caused by gut parasites:
- Abdominal pain around the navel
- Allergies
- Anaemia
- Anxiety that is unexplained
- Appetite: poor in adults, variable in children
- Bloating
- Constipation*
- Diarrhoea
- Fatigue
- Flatulence

- Flushes of heat
- Insomnia
- Irritability
- Itchy nose
- Itchy anus
- Nausea ** (See also Chapter 3)
- Night terrors (in children)***
- Night time fever (mainly in children)
- Pain
- Restless leg syndrome
- Skin itch or 'crawling' sensation
- Teeth grinding
- Weight loss

* Parasites can cause constipation as well as diarrhoea.

**Nausea in people with IBS is most often caused by amoebic parasites, like Giardia.

***Most cases of abdominal pain and 'IBS' in children stem from intestinal parasites or worms of some type. The key symptoms of worms are itchy bottom and/or nose, tummy pain around the navel, unprovoked irritability, teeth grinding and night terrors.

Please note: Children with ongoing diarrhoea, inability to gain weight and who are unresponsive to parasite treatment, should be referred to a medical practitioner for assessment. Ask your doctor to test for Coeliac Disease.

Tests for Parasites

You can have a parasitic infection identified by asking your health professional to order a three-day stool analysis.

For reliable results, stool samples need to be taken over three consecutive days and must be mixed into a special liquid which preserves the parasite eggs. If a stool test is not conducted in this manner, the parasite evidence can degrade before your sample reaches the laboratory.

If you have gut symptoms within two years of having travelled to Africa or South America, you may have uncommon or unusual parasites, in which case there is a special DNA test that shows a wider field of parasite markers. This test may be more appropriate in these cases.

Chapter Two
Treating Intestinal Parasites

Effective treatment for common worms are available from pharmacies, but you may need to repeat the treatment monthly. Some gut parasites are stubborn and require stronger and more specific treatment to remove. Many of the parasites that cause IBS are amoebic or protozoal. When this is the case, usual worming treatments will not be effective.

There is also an anti-parasitic herbal treatment formula developed by Canadian naturopath, the late Dr Hulda Clarke.[6]

- Black Walnut Hull
- Citrus seed
- Clove
- Garlic
- Wormwood (Artemisia Vulgaris)

These herbs help with some parasites, some of the time. The formula is available from health food stores, herbalists and some health professionals.

6 Clark, Hulda Regehr (1995). The Cure for all Diseases, ISBN 9781890035013

Drinking Water

Even in town water supplies, outbreaks of parasites such as *Giardia* and *Cryptosporidium* sometimes occur. Check with your local health authority to see if there has been a recent outbreak of parasites in the water supply. If you use tank water, have it tested for organisms. A good quality ceramic water filter installed in your home will protect you against parasitic outbreaks from both town or tank water. A ceramic dome filter eliminates parasites like Giardia, because the 0.05-micron size of the ceramic pores is smaller than the parasite. You can also use a reverse osmosis water filter. Failing that, boil your drinking water for three to five minutes.

Cina Marinara

The most common and effective therapy that I apply in clinic for parasites is the homeopathic medicine *Cina Marinara 200c*.[7] Take one dose of *Cina Marinara 200c* (5 drops or two pilules) every second day for at least eight weeks. If symptoms improve while patients are taking this medicine, and recur when they stop, it means they need to take it for longer. Some people need to take this medicine for many months. As with all homeopathic medicines, it is safe to take with all prescribed medications and safe for children. *Cina Marinara* can be taken in conjunction with the Clarke herbs mentioned above. In some cases of stubborn parasitic

---

7 *In many countries you can acquire this medicine from a pharmacy, naturopath, or homeopath. See Medicine Supplies, Appendix C.*

infections, the combination gives a better result.

If you do not respond to these measures, you will need professional help. While they can be successfully treated, some parasites such as *Blastocystis hominis, Giardia* and *Dientamoeba fragilis*, often require individualised treatment.

If you improve well on the above recommendations but your symptoms return, it would be best to see a health professional for the next step of your treatment.

See *Finding a Practitioner,* Appendix E.

Chapter Three
'Sluggish Liver'

What does it actually mean to have a 'sluggish liver'? While this naturopathic term is used rather loosely, it refers to a quite specific phenomenon of limited release of bile from the liver.

The term 'sluggish Liver' is used here, because it best describes the concept of a patient's well tested, medically normal liver, yet their digestion and gut function remain troublesome. 'Sluggish liver' can also be described as 'gallbladder, or liver congestion'. The medical term for this is 'biliary tree blockage'. One clinic audit of IBS patients has demonstrated that 60 per cent of patients had undigested fats in their faeces, indicating insufficient bile in the gut.[8]

Sluggish liver, or 'liver congestion' causes a wide range of digestive symptoms and is surprisingly common, especially in young women, who are taking, or have taken the oral contraceptive pill.

8 Dr Braham Rabinov in *www.yourgutfeelings.com.au* (*last accessed 14th February 2019*)

Some people with sluggish liver have a history of gallstones and may have had their gallbladder removed. Even without a gallbladder, sluggish liver can recur over time.

A particular set of symptoms occurs in this group of IBS sufferers who have normal blood results and ultrasounds that do not reveal any gallstones:

Symptoms

- Afternoon headaches
- Chronic (long-standing) constipation
- Dull pain in upper right abdomen
- Flatulence, severe or sudden, usually non-offensive
- Foggy thinking
- Intolerance to fatty, oily or spicy food
- Nausea
- Pale stools
- Skin itch or 'crawling' sensation
- Sudden diarrhoea, even if constipated
- Urgent need for a bowel motion.

Causes

- Heredity
- History of recreational drug use
- Medications, use such as cholesterol-lowering

drugs (Statins.)

- Oral contraceptive pill
- Poor diet
- Zinc deficiency (Zinc helps to prevent toxic accumulations in the liver.)
- None of the above, as the cause cannot be ascertained.

Chapter Four
Treating Sluggish Liver

This is the most straightforward type of IBS to treat. Of all the forms of IBS, sluggish liver responds very well to simple naturopathic liver therapy. Please note that probiotics do not improve this type of IBS.

Herbal Treatment

The fluid extract (**not** tablets or capsules) of the herb Greater Celandine *(Chelidonium Major)* has successfully treated most of my IBS patients with 'sluggish liver'. This medicine starts to relieve symptoms within two to six weeks. See Appendix C for medicine supplies.

The usual adult dose is 10 drops in one tablespoon of water before and after each meal (six times daily). If you feel nauseated after taking a dose, it is a strong indication that their liver needs cleansing! It is not harmful though - just reduce the dose until there is no nausea, then gradually increase the dose until the IBS symptoms improve, without the nausea.

Children

If a child has pale stools, I give this medicine at the following dosage:

> Child 3-8 years: 2 drops in water twice daily.
>
> Child 8-12 years: 5 drops in water twice daily.

Dosage for sensitive people

For patients who are sensitive to medicines in general, begin with one drop only before each meal, and gradually increase the number of drops over a few weeks until symptoms improve. They then stay on that dose for several months.

NOTE! *Patients who have been diagnosed with gallstones **should not take Chelidonium or self treat gallstones.***

Diet

- There are also some dietary ways to help your liver to release more bile:
- Drink strong dandelion root coffee several times daily
- Eat beetroot daily; baked, cooked and sliced, grated, in borscht – any way that you like it.
- Increase your dark green leafy vegetable intake with salads, spinach, and bitter greens such as endive, dandelion greens and radicchio.

- Lemon juice! Squeeze the juice of half a lemon into half a glass of water and drink it ten minutes before and after each meal. Lemon juice may improve, but will not fully correct the problem. Rinse your mouth with plain water afterwards to protect your tooth enamel.

- Limit spicy, oily and fatty foods (fast food, butter, MARGARINE, or fried foods).

- Start vegetable juicing regularly! A juicer is an affordable way of doing your overall health a huge service and you will feel fantastic.

Start each day with a freshly made fruit and vegetable juice.

> 3 medium carrots
> ½ a medium beetroot (tastes surprisingly sweet!)
> 1 stick of celery
> ½ - 1 apple to sweeten your juice
> Fresh ginger according to your taste.
> Ginger enhances the benefit of your juice
>   - and it's also a digestive tonic.

Enjoy! For added benefit, have a second glass later in the day.

Women taking the oral contraceptive pill

If your IBS began after starting the Pill, consider an alternative, non-hormonal form of contraception. Taking the Pill over time will result in zinc depletion: a zinc supplement is needed to improve your liver and gallbladder function. White spots on your fingernails are one common indication of zinc deficiency. Zinc supplements are available in supermarkets, health food shops and pharmacies.

Chapter Five
Yeast Overgrowth

••

Dysbiosis means that the normal, extremely important, micro-organisms in your gut have become out of balance. There are several different types of dysbiosis, but the most common type is 'Candida' (see the box below for other forms of dysbiosis). Candida is a normal gut yeast. When Candida proliferates, it causes a wide range of gut and other symptoms.

Candida requires sugar to survive. People with an overgrowth of Candida often crave sugary, starchy foods. The rapid uptake of sugar by the Candida yeast produces toxic by-products which ultimately worsen, or perpetuate, their symptoms. These symptoms can be *localised* in the gut and cause bloating, pain and flatulence or become *'systemic'* in that they affect the whole body. In adults this can mean mood swings, fluctuating energy levels, ongoing fatigue, and low blood sugar symptoms such as dizziness, shakiness, headaches, food cravings and frequent hunger.

GUT PROBLEMS IN CHILDREN OFTEN GO WITH BEHAVIOURAL ISSUES

In children with gut problems, Candida dysbiosis can cause excessive sugar craving, and refusal to eat anything other than 'white food' like bread, rice, cakes, biscuits and other sweet, starchy food. The effect of fluctuating sugar levels on these children can be excessive wind, bloated tummy, extreme behaviour, violence, inability to concentrate, irritability and hyperactivity, which can easily be mistaken for an attention deficit or behavioural disorder. It is well worth removing sugar and starches from a child's diet and following the dietary guidelines in this chapter before considering medication. Many 'ADHD' children respond extremely well to this type of dietary intervention.

Symptoms

- Abdominal bloating and pain
- 'Allergies' of any kind
- Behaviour problems
- Cravings for sugar and starchy foods – these can be severe, leading children and adults going to extremes to get hold of sugar
- Fatigue
- Flatulence, usually non-offensive
- Headaches

- Joint pains
- Mood swings
- Nappy rash
- Poor concentration
- Skin rashes, especially in skin folds, such as knees, elbows, the groin and under breasts
- Thrush or vaginitis, from babyhood onwards
- Worsening of any symptoms after sugar, white bread, cakes, biscuits, or sugary drinks
- Symptoms which are ongoing and difficult to explain.

Causes of Dysbiosis

- Antibiotics - especially when multiple courses have been given - this includes children who have received antibiotics at birth and/or in the first year of life
- Hormonal imbalance in women
- Poor diet; excessive refined carbohydrates, (white bread, cakes, biscuits, pasta) sugar, beer, soft drinks, sweets
- Oral Contraceptive Pill
- Non-Steroidal anti-inflammatory drugs (NSAIDS)
- Cortisone and other steroid medications.

Chapter Six
Treating Yeast Overgrowth

•••

Since Candida is the most common type of dysbiosis, this is the focus of treatment discussed here.

Diet

The most important treatment for dysbiosis is to remove all sugars and refined carbohydrates from the diet for at least eight weeks.

Be warned; this can be tricky. Withdrawing sugary starchy food from your diet makes you *crave the sugars*. The strength of your sugar craving is equal to the seriousness of your Candida problem. *Unless you avoid all refined starches and sugars, you will not get better.* Sugars and refined carbohydrates include soft drinks, cakes, white bread, white pasta, white rice, sweet biscuits, beer, and dried fruit. Candida organisms are nourished by the sugars which these foods provide.

It is *not* usually necessary to withdraw yeast from your diet, (although you may have been asked to do so by your health professional).

*Examples of **un**refined, **un**processed (whole) foods are:* wholemeal pasta, brown rice, wholemeal crackers, and 100% wholemeal bread.

NB: 'Bread making flour' on labels = white flour.

Golden Rules for Treating Candida

- **Avoid all sugary food, white flour products, commercial breakfast cereals, soft drinks, dried fruit, honey and rice malt.** (Stevia powder and Xylitol are safe, natural sweeteners to use), but *avoid the usual artificial sweeteners.*

- Eat regularly – every two to three hours

- 100 per cent whole grains; wholemeal bread, brown rice, wholemeal pasta

- Have protein with each snack or meal

- Fresh fruit is OK, *but only with protein.* For example, apple with cheese

- The FODMAP diet, shown in Appendix A, helps *this* type of IBS.

If you get hypoglycaemic symptoms (hunger with weakness and dizziness between meals) eat a protein-based snack every two hours throughout the day and have a similar snack at bedtime.

Children

More regular meals can make a real difference to some children's behaviour – give them some protein when their behaviour deteriorates. Do not be concerned about giving your child too much meat. Children need good protein at each meal. The reason for childhood obesity is not because of meat, it is because of too many starchy carbohydrates in the diet, which can also be the beginning of gut problems later in life.

Protein foods are:

- Cheese
- Chicken
- Eggs
- Fish – fresh, or tinned – sardines, mackerel and salmon are best
- Legumes (peas, beans & lentils); dips like hummus are a good way to have legumes
- Meat
- Nuts
- Yoghurt (unsweetened – add fresh fruit if you like).

Examples of protein-based snacks are:

- Hummus or a bean dip with carrot and celery sticks
- Caesar salad – (ask for the egg on top)
- Wholemeal crackers, cheese and fruit
- Green salad and fish with brown rice or wholemeal bread
- Chicken and salad sandwich (wholemeal bread)
- Tub of plain, **unsweetened** yoghurt. Sweeten with fresh fruit only.

To make sure you are getting 100% wholemeal products, read the labels, as product names can be misleading. Buying from a health food or organic store helps you to become familiar with real 100 per cent whole grain products. The extra cost means extra nutrition, particularly in B vitamins and fibre. This can be more economical than you may think, because whole grains are more satisfying and so you need less of them.

Probiotics

Probiotics can really help with Candida-related IBS, but will not help much with other forms of IBS.

It is best to start with small amounts of probiotics and increase slowly. If you have capsules, take one per day. If you have powder, take ½ teaspoon daily. After a few days, increase up to the maximum recommended dose and continue taking the product for several months. Returning symptoms when you stop taking probiotics are a sure sign that you need to keep taking them.

Cheap and easy probiotics in your diet

If you tolerate dairy, you can make your own yoghurt using *kefir*. See Appendix F. Kefir yoghurt is a 'super food' which is superior to commercial probiotics and yoghurts. It can be made at home for the cost of the milk used in making it, instead of up to $50 per container of probiotics. You can buy kefir grains online, or check at your local health food store.

If you are sensitive to dairy products, you can use goats milk, coconut milk or rice milk (not long-life) to make delicious kefir yoghurt. As with probiotic supplements, start with just a couple of teaspoons of kefir at first, and increase after a few days as tolerated. *Too much too soon can aggravate your symptoms*, because the probiotic organisms compete with the candida yeast for territory: you don't want to start a battle in your gut.

Other ways to get probiotics in your diet

Sauerkraut, or pickled cabbage, aids digestion and develops good gut bacteria. Eat a few tablespoons or more with lunch and dinner. If you don't like the taste, mix it with your mashed potatoes, **but don't let it heat up**, as heat will kill the beneficial bacteria. Eating this simple food daily could go a long way to improving your IBS.

You do need to make sauerkraut yourself though, because commercially available sauerkraut may have been pasteurised, which will kill the very bacteria that you need. There are many types of sauerkraut. The Internet is laden with recipes on how to make it. Basically, it involves pounding the head of a cabbage mixed with some salt and letting it ferment. See Sauerkraut recipes in Appendix F.

Medicines

Many patients need specific medicines to fully recover from Candida dysbiosis. These (homeopathic) medicines are the most common ones I prescribe and can safely be used alongside your medications.

- Lycopodium 30c – 1 dose every 2nd day
- Candida albicans 10M – 1 dose daily
- I give both remedies for at least four weeks.

See your practitioner if your symptoms do not begin to improve.

Note: When using homeopathic medicines you are more likely to meet with success if a health professional with homeopathic expertise supervises your progress.

For Medicine Supplies, see Appendix C.

Chapter Seven
Small Intestine Bacterial
Overgrowth
(SIBO)

As well as yeast overgrowth, equally common is another bacterial overgrowth, Small Intestine Bacterial Overgrowth (SIBO).

As with the yeast overgrowth, the normal bacteria become too plentiful, due to a lack of other beneficial bacteria. There are many types of SIBO bacteria but the common ones which cause symptoms are:

- *Klebsiella*
- *Citrobacter*

To be clear: these bacteria are normal residents of the colon, but have opportunistically over-colonised the small intestine, for these reasons:

- Beneficial bacteria have become denuded, through poor diet of excessive sugars and starchy carbohydrates.

- Multiple courses of antibiotics over time have destroyed too much beneficial bacteria, so the residents of the large intestine have moved upstairs into the small intestine and dominated.

- Prolonged stress. Of all the body organs affected by stress, it is the gut which most commonly bears the brunt. People even describe how feelings affect them: "That really kicked me in the gut", "I have a gut feeling about this", "It's a pain in the arse" etc.

- Stress has been shown to disadvantageously affect the gut flora.

SIBO Symptoms

- Bloating
- Constipation
- Diarrhoea
- Flatulence
- Nausea
- Sugar cravings
- Upper abdominal cramping

In severe, longstanding SIBO, you can develop what is popularly known as 'Leaky Gut Syndrome'. Here, due to constant low-grade inflammation caused by the overgrowth, the bowel wall becomes more permeable, and particles of undigested food pass through the gut wall into the bloodstream, rather than being completely digested and eliminated by the gut.

When you have leaky gut, you experience other general symptoms as well as the IBS symptoms:

- Dizziness
- Headache
- Joint pain
- Mood swings
- Poor concentration

These symptoms usually occur after eating sugar and starchy carbohydrates, sometimes even fruit. The bacteria need these foods to survive, and can the the underlying cause of sugar and carbohydrate cravings.

Leaky gut is discussed further in Chapter Nine.

Tests:

- *Complete Digestive Stool Analysis* shows the functional contents of your gut, where lab specialists can determine the type of dysbiosis, and observe indicators for leaky gut syndrome.

- *Gut Permeability test* - a urine test which diagnoses leaky gut syndrome.

- *SIBO Breath test.* This test the gold standard for diagnosing SIBO.

Chapter Eight
Treating Small Intestine Bacterial Overgrowth (SIBO)

•••

If you read through the treatment guidelines for *Yeast Overgrowth in Chapter Five,* you will see that the same rules apply, including removing dietary sugar and starch, having regular protein, and quality probiotic foods.

Additionally, when treating SIBO, it is helpful to use herbal remedies to reduce the bacterial overgrowth, which are listed below. In some SIBO cases, even though antibiotic use may have caused the SIBO, a course of antibiotics may also improve their SIBO symptoms. When the excessive bacteria resided only in the large intestine, previous courses of antibiotics have not been able to reach them. Once these bacteria move up into the small intestine, antibiotics are able to access and decrease the bacterial overgrowth.

Herbs used to treat SIBO:

Although they can be taken in liquid or tablet form, enteric coated capsules are preferred to ensure delivery to the small intestine.

- Garlic
- Oregano Oil
- Clove Oil
- Thyme Oil
- Peppermint Oil
- Berberine, from barberry, or from phellodendron

Chapter Nine
Leaky Gut Syndrome

People with long standing dysbiosis can go on to develop a 'leaky gut' – a condition that can cause severe food sensitivities.

'Leaky gut' means that the wall of your gut becomes too permeable to food particles. These particles which should normally stay in your gut to be excreted, find their way through the gut wall into your bloodstream.

When symptoms occur soon after eating, it is a sure sign of a leaky gut. These symptoms can include mood changes, skin rashes, headaches, fatigue and a foggy head.

Leaky gut can also allow environmental toxins and/or parasites to get into the bloodstream.

Treatment

The first and essential treatment for Leaky Gut Syndrome is to remove the food triggers. A skilled practitioner is needed to identify and help to remove your food triggers so that your gut can heal. Successful treatment results in you becoming less reactive to foods and tolerating a greater variety of foods over time.

Leaky gut responds well to L-Glutamine powder, either loose or encapsulated. This can be mixed with probiotic powder, or a reliable probiotic food: see Chapter Five where probiotics are discussed.

When there is ongoing inflammation of the gut wall, adding other herbs such as golden seal, liquorice, marshmallow and aloe vera, will help to reduce the gut inflammation.

Tests

A specific urine test, available through your health professional, can identify Leaky Gut Syndrome. This is called the *Intestinal Permeability Test*.

Food sensitivities can be identified via an IgG food panel - a blood test that your health professional can arrange for you.

Specific, specialised tests are needed to identify environmental toxins and parasites.

Chapter Ten
Food Sensitivity

Dealing with food sensitivity is best done under the care of a health professional, but if you are sensitive to just one or two foods, and you're able to clearly identify them, you might be able to significantly help your IBS symptoms by eliminating those foods.

Many patients with IBS have some level of food sensitivity. Once identified, removing a problem food can improve your IBS symptoms relatively quickly.

Food sensitivity is ***not allergy***. Allergic reactions cause an immediate reaction to a food, with symptoms like gut pain, bloating, headaches, hot flushing, mood changes and unexplained fatigue. More serious or anaphylactic reactions can cause redness, swelling and breathing difficulty. These can be life-threatening and need immediate medical attention. If you suspect that you have allergic reactions to food, see your doctor for allergy testing. This involves skin scratch and blood tests.

In relation to IBS, this book refers to food <u>sensitivity</u> only.

Food **sensitivity** reactions can be difficult to detect without specific blood tests, because they are usually mild and may not cause symptoms for days or weeks. As well as gut symptoms, food sensitivities can cause sinusitis, nose discharge, chronic cough and eczema, to name a few.

From experience, I can say that it is much easier and more accurate to identify sometimes multiple food sensitivities by having a test called the IgG (Immunoglobulin G4) food sensitivity panel. This is a simple blood test that can be ordered by your practitioner. The result lists the foods to which you have shown an immune reaction. Simply removing the offending foods, for a minimum of three months, can bring good relief, ***provided that it is the main cause of your IBS***. However, food sensitivity may be just one factor contributing to your IBS. Any of the causes of IBS already discussed need to be addressed in order to correct your food sensitivity. For example, most people with food sensitivity will have some degree of gut dysbiosis (see Chapter 7). Therefore, both causes must be treated.

The most common food sensitivities are egg, dairy products, including goat and sheep, wheat (including bread and pasta), yeast, salicylates, yeasts and nuts. For food alternatives to wheat and dairy, see Appendix B.

While food sensitivity is not a life sentence, strict avoidance of the specific foods that affect you in an 'exclusion diet', plus correcting the causes of IBS, can correct food sensitivity. This is good news if you've been told you will "just have to live with" your food sensitivities.

Causes of food sensitivity

Specific food sensitivity can arise from health incidents, like food poisoning. Sensitivity to the offending food can persist after you have recovered from the bout of food poisoning even if before then you could easily tolerate that particular food. It may also be necessary to address gut parasites (see Chapter 1).

Chapter Eleven
Low Gastric Acid
(Hypochlorhydria)

•••

Low stomach acid is an under-acknowledged phenomenon. 'Hypochlorhydria' or low gastric (stomach) acid prevents proper breakdown of the food you have just eaten. It is easily confused with its opposite problem: too much gastric acid, because low gastric acid can cause the symptoms of heartburn.

NOT TOO *MUCH* ACID,
BUT ACID IN THE ***WRONG PLACE***

Here's how it occurs:

> Insufficient stomach acid
>
> ▼
>
> Too much gas produced in the stomach
>
> ▼
>
> Gas applies pressure to the cardiac orifice
> (opening between stomach and oesophagus)
>
> ▼
>
> Acid rises up through the cardiac orifice
>
> ▼
>
> Acid rises into the oesophagus causing 'heartburn'

*This sequence of digestive events means that you have hypochlorhydria (low stomach acid) **with reflux.** Reflux is discussed in the next chapter.*

Symptoms of low gastric acid

- Abdominal bloating
- Belching
- Cold feeling in the stomach soon after eating
- Full sensation in the stomach, even after eating small amounts
- Heaviness in the stomach.

As well as causing heartburn, low stomach acid predisposes to dysbiosis (Chapter 5), by allowing the *overgrowth* of unfriendly yeasts and/or bacteria in the gut.[9]

9 Galland, L, MD 'Intestinal Dysbiosis and the Causes of Disease' www.healthy.net/Health/Article/Intestinal_Dysbiosis_and_the_Causes_of_Disease/423/1 (last accessed 14th February 2019)

Chapter Twelve
Treating Low Gastric Acid

••

Digestive Enzymes

A digestive enzyme supplement that contains at least 300mg of *betaine hydrochloride* will improve digestion caused by low gastric acid. Take one tablet with each meal.

Apple Cider Vinegar

Take ½ teaspoon of apple cider vinegar in ½ glass of water, 30 minutes after each meal.

NOTE: If you get heartburn from either of the above suggestions, it is *unlikely that you have hypochlorhydria*.

You may have *hyperchlorhydria* (**too much** stomach acid) or an inflammatory condition. Stop both supplements and seek advice from your health care practitioner.

Careful of Antibiotics

Antibiotics used to treat amoebic infections like Giardia, Dientamoeba or Blastocystis, can cause or aggravate gastric reflux or heartburn symptoms, and further affect gastric acid.

Chapter Thirteen
Reflux
Gastro-Oesophageal Reflux Disease
'GORD' ('GERD' in USA)

• •

ALL REFLUXES ARE NOT EQUAL

- Is your stomach producing too much acid (the common theory) and causing your reflux? *Maybe.*

- Is your stomach acid just in the wrong place at the wrong time? *Possibly.*

- Do you think that the acid suppressant medication is solving your problem? *Not if when you miss taking your medication the symptoms return.*

What does reflux have to do with IBS? These two conditions are intimately connected and very often the correct treatment given for the underlying cause – let's say sluggish liver – will correct both the reflux and the IBS.

Reflux is a very common ailment, with 22 per cent of IBS

patients suffering from it.[10] Many people have to take their acid-suppressing medication every day otherwise they get heartburn. Some of the trade names of acid-suppressing medications are: *Nexium, Pariet, Somac* and *Zantac*.

In reflux, stomach acid rises up into the oesophagus, causing the all too familiar burning feeling. Reflux can also occur without burning and the only symptom may be a gravelly voice, tickly cough or lump in the throat.

Some people who have reflux may also have a hiatus hernia, a weakening of the diaphragm at the gastro-oesophageal junction. This may or may not be the cause of your reflux, as hiatus hernia can cause many symptoms. Whatever the cause of your reflux, the recommendations in this chapter may offer you relief.

The important thing to know is that reflux is a symptom *arising from a specific* 'cause' that needs to be clearly identified, and then treated.

Reflux Symptoms (irrespective of the cause)

- Cough, or an annoying tickle in the throat, worse when lying down
- Gravelly voice
- **Heartburn**
- Regurgitation of food
- Tight feeling or lump in the throat.

10 Dr Braham Rabinov www.yourgutfeelings.com.au (last accessed 14th February 2019)

Causes of reflux

Let's look at some of the main reasons why reflux occurs. Despite the many different causes, orthodox treatment (acid suppressant medication) is the same for *all types* of reflux. These medications may improve the heartburn *associated with* reflux, but they do not necessarily treat the underlying reason for it.

Hyperchlorhydria (Excessive Stomach Acid)

When you have over-acidity there is a creamy, thick coating on your tongue.

Starchy, sugary and acidic foods will make your symptoms worse. You possibly eat too much meat, pasta, cakes and bread. Your system needs 'alkalising'. You need the alkaline foods, all fruit and vegetables in greater proportion. See Chapter 12.

Hypochlorhydria (Low Stomach Acid)

In low stomach acid, you have burping, heaviness in the stomach and flatulence immediately after eating. Due to insufficient acid, there is so much gas produced that this gas pushes up into the cardiac orifice causing it to allow stomach acid to rise into the oesophagus. This is not a case of too much, but insufficient acid, which then ends up in your oesophagus (the wrong place) and causes burning. Acid suppressant medications work to relieve this 'heartburn', yet the burping and flatulence gets worse over time, because the essential problem is not being addressed. See Chapter 9.

Sluggish Liver

If this is your problem you will have reflux after eating any food which is fatty, oily or spicy. Deep fried food, curries, creamy sauces, will bring on your reflux.
See Chapter 3.

Food Sensitivity

Some people have long undiagnosed food sensitivity (not allergy). It takes exceptional detective work to recognise all the food sensitivities in one person and most people are unable to recognise more than one or two of their own food sensitivities. The only accurate way to diagnose food sensitivity is with a blood test called the *IgG Food Sensitivity Panel*: see Chapter 8.

Stress

Emotional stress has a huge effect on the digestive system, especially upon those who suffer from reflux. There's no point eating your meal if you are trying to solve tomorrow's work problem. This may sound humdrum, but you have to chew your food slowly and completely to digest your food properly. Chewing food well helps to stimulate digestive juices and is conducive to proper digestion.

Globus

Another cause of reflux is a stress-related condition called 'globus' which produces a feeling of a lump in the throat, with difficult swallowing and/or breathing. Sometimes there is heartburn, other times not. *Globus* is more a neurological disturbance than a digestive one, yet is also easily treated with the right medicine. While acid suppressant medications can give relief for the reflux symptoms, these medications do not usually help the symptoms of *globus*.

Rumination Syndrome

Another unusual variant of reflux is Rumination Syndrome. One suffers from repeated, painless regurgitation of food, without any warning. Unfortunately this syndrome does not respond to the normal medications used to treat GORD. For this situation you will need to see a health professional.

Chapter Fourteen
Treating Reflux

The following measures will only reduce the symptoms of reflux. To treat the underlying cause, go to the chapters indicated. Continue with your prescribed medication until symptoms improve.

Caution: *Most over-the-counter antacids contain aluminium, and should not be used long-term. Aluminium is excreted via the kidneys and should be avoided in kidney disease. Aluminium is also associated with Alzheimer's Disease and osteoporosis.*

Heartburn

For prompt relief, take ½ teaspoon of bicarbonate of soda in a small glass of water. After some initial belching most people will get relief.

Reducing Excess Stomach Acid (Hyperchlorhydria)

It is important to maintain a predominantly alkaline diet. All fruit and vegetables are alkaline forming. All starches, fats and proteins are acid forming. Therefore eat more fresh fruit and vegetables every day than meat and grains. A daily fresh vegetable juice of carrot, celery, apple and ginger is a great way to alkalise your system.

Stress

Stress can certainly stimulate too much stomach acid. Eating regular meals and having frequent breaks from work is conducive to proper digestion.

Nutritional Deficiency

Nutritional deficiency plays a part in the acid/alkaline balance. Calcium, magnesium, sodium and potassium are alkaline minerals and are abundant in all fruit and vegetables. Depleted stores of these minerals caused by poor diet and/or prolonged stress, can lead to a hyper-acidic system. There is a place for mineral supplementation in hyperacid conditions, but these should be prescribed by your health professional.

Food sensitivity

Before turning to antacid medication, I strongly recommend that long-term reflux sufferers eliminate the possibility of specific food sensitivities by taking an IgG blood test.

The treatment for food sensitivity-induced reflux is complete removal of the trigger foods for at least three months. Simply avoiding specific foods according to your blood test often results in rapid improvement of reflux symptoms.

Tissue Salts (Biochemic, or Dr Schuessler Salts)

These simple tissue salts are easily available in pharmacies and health food stores. For acidity, Nat Phos 6x taken 3 times daily can help in modifying-over acidity. Tissue salts can be taken in conjunction with any other prescribed medication.

Globus

The most common and effective medicine I use to treat globus is the homeopathic remedy Ignatia 200c. One dose taken once every 2nd day for at least six weeks, often solves the problem.

Inflammatory Disorders

While the above measures may improve reflux, they will not necessarily heal inflammation, so do not use them to treat any of these conditions:

- Duodenitis (inflammation of the duodenum)
- Gastritis (inflammation of the stomach)
- Oesophagitis (inflammation of the oesophagus)
- Peptic ulcer.

Chapter Fifteen
When there is More Than One Cause of IBS

Unfortunately for many IBS sufferers, there will never be a single treatment for all cases of IBS. The reason for this is that gut parasites, reduced bile production and dysbiosis can all occur either separately or together. Multiple causes create a complex of IBS symptoms that need to be treated.

This highlights the importance of identifying one or more of the underlying pathologies of **each case** of IBS to effectively treat them. Food sensitivities indicate the need to treat gut parasites, liver function, dysbiosis, leaky gut and so on. Checking and treating each of these causes can be done progressively, over a few months, and will lead to a far better outcome, rather than just treating the presenting symptoms, which does not produce satisfactory outcomes. In this way, IBS can be resolved (not just managed) in a far shorter period of time, than the many years, or even decades, that people are left suffering with their digestive issues.

It is frustrating for me to hear patients say that they have been told there is no cure for IBS, that they will just have to live with it; and learn to manage their stress. It's frustrating for them because they have to live with their symptoms; and it's frustrating for me because I know it's not true.

IBS can be resolved, no matter how long a person has suffered from it. The important aspect is to work out which of the many causes applies. Once the cause(s) is correctly identified, the treatment is generally straightforward. Remember that dietary changes alone do not resolve IBS, it is the appropriate treatment that will resolve gut reactivity and the symptoms associated with it.

Chapter Sixteen
What if None Of This Fits You?

Only the most common types of IBS are covered in this book. If none of the information provided here seems to fit your symptoms, it's time to do some specialised pathology tests.

These are:

- Complete Digestive Stool Analysis (identifies parasites, bacterial overgrowth or undergrowth, yeasts and digestive enzymes)

- Mineral analysis, which identifies toxic elements like copper and mercury. High levels of these elements are often found in severe cases of IBS. Mineral analysis can be assessed using a sample of hair, or via spectrophotometry from some health professionals.

- IgG Food Sensitivity Panel (clearly identifies which foods are causing symptom reactions).

These tests must be ordered and interpreted by a health professional.

Chapter Seventeen
When To Seek a Second Opinion

When a person is unresponsive to all IBS treatments (including the ones in this book) they may have to revisit their 'IBS' diagnosis. If you have any of the symptoms below, it may be time to seek a second opinion. Make sure you alert your health professional to any of the symptoms below:

SYMPTOM	POSSIBLE CAUSE / TESTS NEEDED
Anxiety that's unexplained	Gut problems related to thyroid disorder
Failure to thrive in children	Coeliac disease*
Fatty stools (mushy, pale stools that float)	Metabolic disturbance including pancreatic disorder
Fever with gut symptoms	Fever is not caused by IBS
Heart racing	Thyroid disorder
Ongoing loss of appetite	Iron or vitamin B12 deficiency, other illness

SYMPTOM	POSSIBLE CAUSE / TESTS NEEDED
Ongoing pain anywhere in your digestive tract	Other condition; not all gut pain is caused by IBS
Persistent flushing of the face	Inflammatory bowel disease
Persistent iron deficiency anaemia	Possible bleeding in the gut
Persistent mouth ulcers	Inflammatory bowel disease
Regular blood in your bowel motions	Bleeding always needs a full investigation
Skin lesions appearing suddenly	Inflammatory bowel disease
Sudden change in bowel habits – (constipation, diarrhoea, pain) without explanation	All sudden bowel changes require full medical investigation
Unusual heat intolerance	Thyroid disorder
Unexplained vomiting *(This is not a symptom of IBS)*	Full medical investigation
Unexplained weight loss	Prompt medical investigation

*Coeliac Disease

Up to three per cent of patients diagnosed with IBS are found to have Coeliac Disease. Coeliac disease is an inflammatory bowel disease, as opposed to IBS which is a functional bowel disease – very different! A simple blood test to confirm this diagnosis, followed by a biopsy of the gut wall, can save years of suffering.

Chapter Eighteen
What Next?

••

Whether you have suffered from IBS for one or 20 years, it makes no difference to the treatment outcome. By discovering your cause(s) of IBS, the information given here will enable you to see real improvement in your IBS symptoms. As you can see, IBS solutions are not 'one size fits all.' And no single treatment can benefit every IBS sufferer. This is the common mistake made by health professionals: they attempt to boil down IBS into one entity. It is not!

Nor is IBS caused by the food you are eating. Special exclusion diets may have the place, but they do not address the essential IBS causes in an integral way.

If you are not seeing improvement, I realise how truly disheartening it can be that yet another strategy you've tried has failed. *However, it does not mean that you cannot be helped: please be aware that there are uncommon types of IBS not mentioned here, and combinations of causes that may be tricky for you to recognise in yourself or your family member.*

Provided you have had a proper medical diagnosis, seeing a practitioner familiar with these methods is a natural next step. In Australia, I have trained and accredited practitioners who are listed at www.irritablebowelsyndrome.net.au . Distance consultations are available where needed.

I wish you the best possible recovery from your IBS.

APPENDICES

Appendix A
The FODMAPS Diet

•••

Essentially, this diet isolates the food groups that aggravate some forms of IBS. There are many references to FODMAPS diets available on the Internet, but here is an overview.

There are four broad classes of FODMAP foods:

- Oligosaccharides
- Disaccharides
- Monosaccharides
- Polyols

This rather restricted diet offers real benefits, for those with either Candida or Bacterial dysbiosis. (See Chapter 5) People with this type of IBS benefit from a combination of FODMAPS exclusions and recolonisation of the gut with probiotics and digestive enzymes. Recolonisation of the gut will result in reduced dependence on the FODMAPS diet.

However helpful the FODMAP diet is, in my experience it does not address the underlying cause(s). Resolving IBS requires diagnosis of the causes:

- Which of the common causes described above do you have?
- Do you have any food sensitivities?

The answer to these questions is the place to begin your IBS treatment.

FODMAPS Food Exclusions

Oligosaccharides

- *Fructans* may interfere with absorption of fructose, thus aggravating symptoms in fructose malabsorption. Fructans-rich foods are: artichokes (globe), artichokes (Jerusalem), asparagus, beetroot, chicory, dandelion leaves, garlic (in large amounts), leek, onion (brown, white, Spanish, onion powder), radicchio lettuce, spring onion (white part), wheat (in large amounts), rye (in large amounts),

- *Galactans* act much like fructans. The main galactans-rich foods are legumes (soy, baked beans, kidney beans, borlotti beans, chickpeas, lentils), cabbage and Brussels sprouts.

Disaccharides

- *Lactose* (milk sugar) is found in dairy products, chocolate and other sweets, pre-prepared soups and sauces. Lactose is poorly absorbed if you are lactose intolerant.

Monosaccharides

- Fructose (fruit sugar). Fructose is often added to commercial foods and drinks as high fructose corn syrup (HFCS). Fructose can cause symptoms even in healthy people. Fructose is found in honey, dried fruits (prunes, figs, dates, raisins) apples, pears, sweet cherries, peaches, agave syrup, watermelon and papaya.

- *Sorbitol* as in "sugar-free chewing gum"and "low calorie foods"; Sorbitol is found naturally in stone fruits (peaches, apricots and plums).
- *Xylitol* naturally appears in some berries. A pack of chewing gum containing sorbitol or xylitol may cause bloating or diarrhoea even in healthy people.

Polyols

Polyols, also known as sugar alcohols, appear as artificial sweeteners in commercial foods and drinks. Polyols are found in apples, apricots, avocados, cherries, longans, lychees, nectarines, pears, plums, prunes and mushrooms. The following food additives are all polyols:

Arabitol, Erithrytol, Glycerol, Glycol, Isomalt, Lactitol, Maltitol (965), Mannitol (421), Ribitol, Sorbitol (420) Xylitol (967)

FODMAPS BOOKLET

You can download a booklet on the FODMAPS diet from the Eastern Health Clinical School at Monash University, Melbourne, Victoria, Australia from www.monashfodmap. com/i-am-a-health-professional/fodmap-resources/ (Last accessed 14th February 2019)

Appendix B
Gluten, Dairy, Egg and Yeast Free

••

Here's a brief look at some common food sensitivities:

Gluten

Gluten is found in: wheat (bread, cake, biscuits, pasta) rye, barley, oats plus a range of sauces and gravies. Careful label checking is needed.

Gluten-free grains include:
Rice, corn (maize), soya bean, tapioca, chia, buckwheat, millet, amaranth, sorghum, quinoa, arrowroot.

For the best information on gluten free diets, websites about coeliac disease provide detailed dietary information.

Dairy

'Dairy' foods include all animal milks; cow, goat and sheep and their products of cheese, yoghurt, butter and cream.

Some people are able to tolerate goat's milk in preference to cow's milk. Dairy products occur in a range of baked goods, including breads, so label checking is necessary.

Dairy free products include:
Soy milk, rice milk, oat milk, almond milk, coconut cream and coconut milk. Soy cheese is also available.

Eggs

Eggs are found in a wide range of baked goods, including breads – *especially* 'gluten free' breads, so be sure to carefully check labels. 'Egg replacers' are available.

Yeast

Yeast is found in:
Bread, Beer, Vegemite, Bonox, Marmite or similar spreads.
Yeast free breads are available in health food stores and some supermarkets.

Appendix C
Medicine & Supplement Supplies
••

Local health food stores, pharmacies and supermarkets have a wide range of products and supplements.

Your local naturopath or homeopath can supply herbal and homeopathic medicines.

Medicines mentioned throughout this book are easily available via the Internet.

Appendix D
Constipation

Most of the time, constipation is the *result* of one of the causes of IBS discussed in this book.

Even if you have a bowel motion every day, it is easy to assume that you are not constipated. The average adult should pass a "sausage" 2 to 3 cm in diameter, and 12 cm in length, every day. After the motion, you should feel a calm, satisfied feeling. Not having a pleasant feeling after a motion may mean that, even if you have a regular bowel motion, you are constipated. If you have constipation-dominant IBS, your pain will be worse before you move your bowels and *better afterwards*.

NB: *Diarrhoea is sometimes a symptom of constipation.* Rather than being a true diarrhoea, it can be 'constipation with overflow.' The reason for this is that faeces are actually firmly packed in your bowel, and only some of this can be evacuated, sometimes with a loose motion. It is the bowel's natural response to a congested bowel, to produce unformed loose stools as a means to properly evacuating the bowel.

Symptoms of constipation, or 'faecal loading' are:

- Loose motions with a 'never completely empty' feeling after going to the toilet.

- Dull, achy pain often in the upper right abdomen
- Unable to have a normal bowel motion when the urge occurs.

If your IBS mysteriously vanished for a week after having a colonoscopy, this is almost diagnostic of chronic constipation. The bowel preparation has fully cleared your bowel, but after a week or so the old symptoms creep back.

Why are you constipated?

By the time you seek treatment for your IBS, most people have self-prescribed a laxative or two. Constipation can be a result of any of the IBS causes discussed in the early chapters of this book.

Common 'lifestyle' reasons for constipation:

- Inadequate fluid intake (adults should drink eight glasses of water daily, plus one extra glass for every glass of tea, coffee or alcoholic beverage, since all of these are diuretics)
- Poor diet, lacking in fruit, vegetables and fibre.
- Insufficient exercise
- Delaying going to the toilet; being too busy, particularly first thing in the morning. This habit alone is often triggers the IBS symptom picture. Some school children won't go to the toilet for the whole day to avoid the embarrassment of going at school – a habit that can last into adulthood.

Symptoms of constipation caused by **haemorrhoids**:

First, see a medical practitioner to have your haemorrhoids properly diagnosed.

- An occasional smear of normal coloured blood after a motion.
- Pain in the rectum during or after a motion.
- A 'stop start' nature of passing a motion.
- The motion feels too big to pass.

The recommendations below will help reduce the size of your haemorrhoids; the less straining, the more they have a chance to heal.

Basic Treatment

The object of all these measures is to remove your abdominal discomfort for a relaxing, completely empty feeling at least once a week.

Laxatives and bulking agents, such as Psyllium powder, have their place, but for many people do not solve the problem in the long term.

- Drink at least eight glasses of water daily
- 3 pieces of fresh fruit plus 5 serves of vegetables daily
- Beans, peas and lentils every day or every second day. (Bean salad, bean dip, Indian dahl, falafel)
- Prunes and/or prune juice daily

Fresh juice each morning:

- 3 medium size carrots
- ½ a medium size, raw beetroot (tastes surprisingly sweet)
- 1 stick of celery
- Ginger and/or apple to taste.

If the above measures do not help after 1-2 weeks, try a **deliberate "clean out" once each week**, when you are able.

Steps for your clean out, starting with the gentlest method first:

- For 24 hours eat fresh fruit only; any type of fruit whenever you feel hungry.
- Drink as much water or herbal tea as you can for the whole day.
- Acquire a magnesium powder or Milk of Magnesia from your local pharmacy. Magnesium Oxide is the best. Take 2 teaspoons in water every 2 hours for six hours, which should produce several loose, painless motions the next day.
- Drink one glass of water with 2 teaspoons of Epsom salts every two hours for six hours. There should be loose stools over several hours, resulting in a good clean out. However, some people do get cramps from using Epsom salts.

Women:

If your constipation is related to your menstrual cycle please take note:
If you have worsening of constipation at ovulation (mid cycle) or during your menstrual period, with significant abdominal pain, it may be that your "IBS" is a gynaecological problem, not a digestive one. Be sure to mention these symptoms to your doctor.

Appendix E
Finding a Practitioner
· ·

If you have tried the suggestions outlined in this book and met with limited or no success, then it is time to see a practitioner.

Within Australia
Trained and accredited practitioners in Australia, are listed at www.irritablebowelsyndrome.net.au

Outside Australia
There are two options:
Naturopaths, homeopaths and herbalists in your locality all have access to the medicines discussed in this book. They will be able to provide you with medicines in the context of a consultation.

Alternatively, arrange a distance consultation with myself or another practitioner via telephone or Skype. All details are at www.irritablebowelsyndrome.net.au

Appendix F
Making Your Own Probiotics

Probiotic foods are equally effective as commercial probiotics and are easily made at home. They are:

- Kefir yoghurt
- Pickles
- Sauerkraut

Kefir Yoghurt

Organisms Found In Kefir Yoghurt

The range of organisms found in Kefir yoghurt is wider than any probiotic you can purchase. It contains more than thirty types of lactobacilli, acetobacter, streptococci, lactococci and yeasts.

Once you have your own **Kefir grain**, you can make your own yoghurt with fresh milk at room temperature, because it **regenerates perpetually in fresh milk, at room temperature**. Kefir grains do not deteriorate; all that is required is fresh milk of your choice and five minutes of your time each day.

Kefir can be made at **any temperature** from 4 to 40°C. At lower temperatures it will take longer to set.

As soon as you get your grain, put it in half a cup of cow, goat, soy or coconut milk, cover, and leave on the kitchen bench until it thickens. Kefir yoghurt is runnier than commercial yoghurt. As the grain grows, it will set larger quantities of milk. Eventually the grain will grow so that it sets up to one litre of your preferred milk at a time. The first few batches of Kefir you make may not yield as much yoghurt, or taste as good as later, as the grains are "waking up".

How To Make Kefir Yoghurt

Utensils:

- A 500 ml ceramic or glass container with a cover
- A container to store kefir in the fridge
- A sieve to strain the freshly made Kefir

Use ANY type of milk (including coconut, soy, rice milk, powdered, sheep and goats') except long life milks.

Method:

1. Put the Kefir grains in your container, add your preferred milk and cover

2. Add a dessert spoon of milk powder if you prefer thicker yoghurt.

3. Stir every 12 hours or so. Setting time will vary, from one to several days, according to the strength of the grain, room temperature and the type of milk.

4. When set, pour through a sieve, and retain the kefir grain.

5. Spoon unwashed grains back into the 500 ml jar and repeat the process. Wash utensils in **unchlorinated** water.

NB. Never heat the milk, as excess temperature is one of the few things that will kill the grains. Similarly, never use bleaches or detergents for cleaning the utensils you use when making Kefir, as these may kill or taint the grain.

Sharing grains:

When the grains are about the size of a walnut, small pieces drop off readily. A grain the size of 1mm diameter is enough to grow new grains! Take a small grain and grow it for a week in the same jar, then pass it on when it's bigger.

Storing Grains:

Store in the refrigerator in a jar covered with filtered, unchlorinated water. Refresh the water every week.

*USE **CLEAN WATER**: CHLORINATED TOWN WATER MAY DAMAGE THE GRAINS.*

Not Sure How to Start?

Go to Youtube to see a simple demonstration: http://www.youtube.com/watch?v=g8inJzX-6yE

References:

- *Encyclopaedia of Food Science & Food Technology & Nutrition 5 ISBN: 0-12-226855-5, ACADEMIC PRESS -> Food Technology and Nutrition: "Kefir" pp 1804-1808.*

- *International Journal of Systematic Bacteriology 44 (3) 435-439 (1994) [21 ref. En] - * two new organisms recently discovered!*

Other Probiotic Foods:

Kim chi (Korean Sauerkraut) - Makes one quart (1200mls)

1 head Wombok cabbage (also known as Napa, or Chinese cabbage)

1 bunch spring onions, chopped

1 cup grated carrot

½ cup grated daikon radish (optional)

1 tablespoon of freshly grated ginger

3 cloves of garlic, peeled and minced

½ teaspoon of dried chilli flakes

1 teaspoon of salt

4 tablespoons of whey, or one additional teaspoon of salt

Japanese Sauerkraut

1 head Wombok (Napa, or Chinese Cabbage) cored and finely shredded

1 bunch green onions, chopped

2 tablespoons of soya sauce

2 tablespoons of freshly squeezed lemon juice

1 teaspoon of sea salt

2 tablespoons of whey (from making kefir)

If whey is not available, use another teaspoon of salt

Method for both recipes

Put all the ingredients in a bowl and pound with a wooden pounder, meat hammer, or the pestle from a mortar and pestle until there is lots of juice. Place in a one litre wide mouthed glass or ceramic container, and press down firmly until the juice rises above the cabbage, by about one centimetre. There should be a couple of centimetres of space below the top of the container. Cover and leave at room temperature for three days, then store in the fridge.

Salsa Vegetable Pickle (no cooking required)

1 kg tomatoes, 1 capsicum, 1 red onion, 4 cloves of garlic, fresh coriander

1-2 teaspoons chillies (optional)

Wash and chop everything up, mix it all together, pack tightly into a jar, leaving a 1cm space at the top. Cover, but don't seal. In a few days bubbles will start to appear. The jar may overflow, so place it on a plate. When the bubbling settles, seal the jar and it's ready to eat.

To stop further fermentation store in the fridge. Start eating small quantities and gradually increase the amount. Eat within two weeks.

Appendix G
Tests

Some testing may be necessary to find the underlying cause of your IBS.

These include:

- **Coeliac Disease Test:** confirmed by blood test. Further investigations may be necessary.

- **Complete Digestive Stool Analysis**: This three-day stool sample. Tests for parasites, digestive function, gut flora balance.

- **Hair Mineral Analysis**: Assesses nutritional status and the presence of heavy metals, some of which can be the cause of IBS.

- **Oligoscan:** Mineral analysis conducted in consultation via spectrophotometry. To find practitioners in Australasia and South East Asia: www.oligoscan.net.au

- **IgG Food Panel:** Identifies food sensitivities, ordered by your health professional

- **Intestinal Permeability Test**: This urine test identifies Leaky Gut Syndrome. Ordered by your health professional.

About The Author

Jon Gamble trained in osteopathy, naturopathy and homeopathy and has practised Complementary Medicine since 1987. During this time, the prevalence of bowel disorders has rapidly increased, leading Jon to focus on the clinical understanding of the differing presentations of IBS. He has been able to develop unique ways of successfully treating obstinate and distressing gut disorders, using his personally developed combinations of diagnostic methods and treatment protocols.

He is the author of three practitioner books:

- *Accurate Daily Prescribing for a Successful Practice*
- *The Treatment of Irritable Bowel Syndrome*
- *Obstacles to Cure: Toxicity, Deficiency and Infection*

He has also co-authored *Treat Your Child Yourself; A parents guide to Drug Free Solutions for Common Complaints,* with his wife Nyema Hermiston, also a homeopath and naturopath.

Jon's specialty areas of treatment are:

- Digestive diseases
- Paediatrics
- Allergies

- Chronic Fatigue Syndrome.

Jon is an accredited practitioner with:
- Australian Register of Homeopaths (AROH)
- Australian Homeopathic Association (AHA)
- Australian Traditional-Medicine Society (ATMS)

Qualifications

Bachelor of Arts (Monash University)

Diploma of Naturopathy (British College of Naturopathy)

Advanced Diploma of Homeopathy (Sydney College of Homeopathic Medicine)

Websites: www.karunahealthcare.com.au
www.chronicfatiguesyndrome.net.au
www.oligoscan.net.au
www.irritablebowelsyndrome.net.au

Email: info@irritablebowelsyndrome.net.au

Selected Bibliography

Articles

- Daley, J, *"Food Allergy/Intolerance"* in Sarris, J & Wardle, J (eds), *Clinical Naturopathy: An Evidence-Based Guide to Practice,* Churchill Livingstone, Sydney, 2010

- Haresh, K, et al, *Trop Med Int Health,* 1999; 4:274

- Hawrelak, J "Irritable Bowel Syndrome: Constipation-Dominant" in Sarris, J & Wardle, J (eds), *Clinical Naturopathy: An Evidence-Based Guide to Practice,* Churchill Livingstone, Sydney, 2010

- Hawrelak, J, "Gastro-oesophageal Reflux Disease" in Sarris, J & Wardle, J (eds), *Clinical Naturopathy: An Evidence-Based Guide to Practice,* Churchill Livingstone, Sydney, 2010

- Heap, Timothy, "How to Treat: Irritable Bowel Syndrome", *Australian Doctor,* 23.10.98 & 30.10.98

- Hewett, Peter, "How to Treat: Acute Lower Abdominal Pain", *Australian Doctor,* 14.2.03, I-VIII

- Holten, K, et al, "Diagnosing the patient with abdominal pain and altered bowel habits: is it irritable bowel syndrome?" *Am Fam Physician,* 2003; 67: 2157-62

- Holten, K, et al, "Irritable Bowel Syndrome: minimise testing, let symptoms guide treatment", *J Fam Pract,* 2003; 52: 942-50

- Howlett, M & Gibson, P, "Update: Crohn's Disease", *Medical Observer,* 12.12.03, 28-29.

- *International Journal of Systematic Bacteriology* 44 (3) 435-439 (1994) [21 ref. En]

- Jones, J, et al, "British Society of Gastroenterology guidelines for the management of irritable bowel syndrome", *Gut*, 2000; 47 (supp II): ii-19

- Kennedy, T, et al, "Cognitive Behavioural Therapy in addition to antispasmodic treatment for irritable bowel syndrome in primary care: randomised clinical trial", *British Medical Journal* 2005; 331:435

- Ratnaike, Ranjit, "How to Treat: Constipation", *Australian Doctor*, 17.9.99, I-VIII

- Rieger, Nicholas, "How to Treat: Faecal Incontinence", *Australian Doctor*, 6.9.02, I-VII

- Starr, J, "Clostridium difficile associated diarrhoea: diagnosis and treatment", *British Medical Journal* 2005; 331: 498-501

Books

- Brown, H, *Basic Clinical Parasitology*, Appleton-Century-Crofts, 1975.

- Campbell-McBride, N, *Gut and Psychology Syndrome*, Medinform Publishing, Cambridge, UK, 2004

- Satsangi, J & Sutherland, L (eds), *Inflammatory Bowel Disease*, Churchill Livingston, London, 2003

- Guillory, Dr Gm IBS: *A Doctor's Plan for Chronic Digestive Troubles,* 3 ed Hartley & Marks Publishers, Vancouver, 2001

- Sarris, J & Wardle, J (eds), *Clinical Naturopathy: An Evidence-Based Guide to Practice*, Churchill Livingstone, Sydney, 2010

- *Encyclopaedia of Food Science & Food Technology & Nutrition* 5 ISBN: 0-12-226855-5, ACADEMIC PRESS -> Food Technology and Nutrition: "Kefir" pp 1804-1808.

Websites (Last accessed 14th February 2019)

www.cdd.com.au/

www.mdheal.org/leakygut.htm

www.yourgutfeelings.com.au

www.gutfoundation.com.au

www.ksu.edu/parasitology/625tutorials/index.html